ROBERT LEWIS DABNEY
THE PROPHET SPEAKS

Robert Lewis Dabney
The Prophet Speaks

Edited by Douglas W. Phillips

© The Vision Forum, Inc.

All rights reserved. No part of this publication may be reproduced without the prior written permission of the publisher.

Cover photo courtesy of Austin Theological Seminary.

Printed in the United States of America

First printing January, 1997
Second printing October, 2001
Third printing April, 2006

The Vision Forum, Inc.
4719 Blanco Rd.
San Antonio, TX 78212

Table of Contents

Acknowledgement & Dedication ix

Introduction xi
   Dabney's Times xii
   The Man and His Life xiii
   His Views xiv
   Dabney's Legacy xvii

I: Dabney on Education 1
   On How State Education Money Can Corrupt Good People 1
   Just Because the Idea is New Does Not Make It Better 1
   The Evidence Indicates That Government Education is a Flop 2
   Parents Must Privately Control Education 2
   The Pagan Presupposition Behind Compulsory Education 2
   Parents vs. The State 3
   *Government Education Will Lead to an
      Increase in Juvenile Crime.* 3
   Government Education Has a Poor Track Record 3
   Home Education is the Key to Success 4

*Compulsory and Free Education:
  That Which Costs Nothing is Never Valued*................... 4
On the Means of Charity..................................... 4
*Dabney Opposes Bible Reading in Government Schools
  Because He Opposes Government Schools* 5
Only Christian Education is True Education 6
*That Some Survive Government Schools is No Justification for
  Others Taking the Same Course* 7
On How Public Education Will Lead to Woe.................... 7
Dabney On Compulsion and Redistribution of Wealth 8
Dabney Assails Pro-Government-School Protestant Hypocrites .. 8
Dabney Sees Only Three Viable Alternatives for State Education .. 9
Moral Education is Impossible Without Jesus Christ 10
The Common Schools Educate for Sloth, Not for Usefulness 11
*Dabney Opposes using Children as Missionaries in
  Government Schools*.. 11
*Evil Peer-Grouping is Inherent in the
  Government School Classroom*............................... 12
*The Church Does Not Have Jurisdiction to Be the
  Primary Educator of Children*.............................. 12
*If the State Educates, the Education will be
  Manipulated by Partisan Interets* 13
The Public School Teacher is the Agent of the State......... 13
Education Can Not Be Neutral 13

II: Dabney on Politics 15
On Biblical Voting Ethics and Against Slavish Partisan Loyalties .. 15
Christians will be Judged by God if They Vote for the Unjust 16
Do Not Vote for Those who will Unjustly Send Your Sons to War ... 17
Partisan Politics and Political Compromise.................. 17

Compromise 19
The Bible, Not Human Experience, is the Final Authority 19
Republican Government, Not Democracy, Favored by God 20

III: DABNEY ON THE FAMILY 21
A Revival of Fatherhood and Parental Responsibility 21
The Awe of Parenthood 23
The Necessity of Parental Instruction 24
Parental Love is Foundational to a Free Society 25

IV: DABNEY ON FEMINISM & BIBLICAL MANHOOD 27
Women Preachers 27
The Rise of Feminism 27
Paul Was Not a Male Chauvinist 28
Cultural Androgyny 28
The Devastating Consequences of Feminism 29
Women's Rights Will Lead to the Abolition of Marriage 29
The Character of the Children of Feminists 30
Feminism is an Attack Against Femininity 31
The Consequences of Feminism on America as a Nation 33
No-Fault Divorce Will Rise to Prominence Along with Feminism .. 34
The Necessity that Men Embrace True Courage 35
The Battle Rages On 35
Responsibility and Justice 36

APPENDIX 37
Bibliography 37
About the Editor 37

Acknowledgement & Dedication

Almost two decades ago a pioneering Baptist preacher by the name of Lloyd Sprinkle began the monumental task of republishing many of the great but oft ignored Christian writings of the nineteenth century. Since then Sprinkle Press has generated more than forty such volumes, each as relevant today as it was when first penned by its author.

Over the years Sprinkle Press has released many significant volumes, but few have matched the republished works of Robert Lewis Dabney for their ability to challenge and inspire. I will go further: Lloyd Sprinkle and his publishing house is almost single-handedly responsible for a revival of interest in the life and letters of this extraordinary Southern theologian and patriot. Twenty years ago only a handful of academics and avid history buffs were seriously studying the works of this prolific writer. Today the number of Dabney devotees is growing.

It was my great privilege to present at a recent historical conference sponsored by Lloyd Sprinkle a series of lectures on the prophet-like proclamations of Mr. Dabney. Much of this booklet is derived from the research compiled from those lectures.

I wish not only to acknowledge the original dabneyphile, Lloyd Sprinkle, and his immense contribution to the modern revival of interest in the writings of the late great theologian, but to dedicate this volume to my friend, in appreciation for his many years of service to the Body of Christ.

Introduction

Once or twice in every generation a prophet emerges who challenges with devastating accuracy the reigning cultural paradigm. The prophet is that individual who is able to see through the foggy mist of unreason which seeps into a culture that has forgotten its past and rejected the faith of its fathers. While the gods of the age lure the ignorant masses like so many sheep to the precipice of destruction, the prophet beckons them to the safety of solid ground. Even the abyss of intellectual and spiritual bankruptcy, the prophet retains clarity of thought and steadfast devotion to his Maker. He boldly states what many know to be true but few are willing to say. He is a man of reason and faith. He is a proclaimer of truth on a mission to a civilization in decline.

    Such a man was Robert Lewis Dabney. Perhaps no Christian leader of the nineteenth century filled the role of prophet with greater proficiency. In his devotion to the Holy Scriptures, his unwavering commitment to principle, his mastery of logic, and his ability to employ those qualities when addressing the cultural crises of his day, none were his equal. Certainly there were few Christian men of his age with the courage and tenacity to tackle the infidel spirit of that momentous time. He was the quintessential prophet: bold, accurate and unappreciated by those who could most benefit from his prophecy. One hundred years after his death, Dabney's logic remains sound, his conclusions accurate, and his subject-matter relevant.

Dabney's Times

Dabney did most of his writing during the latter part of the second half of the nineteenth century. It was a time of unprecedented changes in the life of the great experiment called America. He spoke to the newly-emerging world of Charles Darwin, Karl Marx, John Dewey and Sigmund Freud. It was in his day that God was divorced from science, Scripture from the university, patriarchy from the family, and the common law from our judicial system. The world of Robert Lewis Dabney was a world dominated by the "-isms" of an intelligent elite who sought to transform society into the image of the god they worshipped: Man. Dabney recognized these dangers as did few others and fought against them with the skill of a master apologist whether they took the form of progressivism, suffragettism, evolutionism, transcendentalism, German higher criticism, or even collectivism. What the intellectuals of his day saw as progress, Dabney saw as cultural suicide. It was at that target that Dabney aimed his pen.

If the modern reader is a bit shocked at the "take no prisoners" attitude exemplified by Mr. Dabney's writing, he must remember that many of the well-established postulates of our time were in Dabney's day just beginning to rise in their ascendancy. The stakes were high. He knew only too well that if these movements and theories were left unchecked and unchallenged to fester like an intellectual canker in the American psyche, the very soul of this once great nation would be sold to the God of the age whose father is that dread author of lies himself. It was the task of the apologist, Dabney believed, to expose, refute and annihilate every attempt to overthrow of Christian culture.

Thus, with the precision of a master surgeon, Dabney focused his intellectual scalpel on the malignant thinking of the liberals of his day, and then proceeded to systematically root out their cancerous reasonings. And yet, not content to remove the surface tumor, Dabney's pen never rested until the great author had sought out and destroyed every cancerous cell of unbiblical, specious, hypocritical, self-serving or inconsistent reasoning presented by the advocates of atheistic progressivism.

The Man and His Life

Who was this man? A comely figure with "keen black eyes" who stood about six feet tall, Robert Lewis Dabney was a person of diverse talents who played many roles in his life of more than eighty years. From mapmaker and architect to financier and farmer, from biographer to poet, his talents and skills were representative of the sort of well-rounded and eclectic training which typified the Virginia gentlemen of the previous century. But the tow roles for which he is best known are that of theologian and soldier.

Dabney had a long and distinguished career serving at Union Seminary and stood beside Thornwell, Palmer, and Girardau as one of the great thinkers of the Southern Presbyterians. Prior to the War Between the States, Dabney had been a voice of moderation to the people of Virginia pleading with his Southern brethren to avoid secession and war. But once the war began, and in the years that followed its conclusion, few men proved to be more articulate in their defense of the South than Dabney. Despite the fact that Dabney had never received a military education, the great Stonewall Jackson personally offered Dabney the position as his Chief of Staff, with the privilege of doing missionary work in the army every Sunday. Though he suffered from constant illness, Dabney valiantly served beside Jackson during the Shennandoah Valley Campaign.

Dabney was a man of extraordinary principle whose character

remained unblemished throughout a long and distinguished career. As with most good prophets he was accused at various times of being unnecessarily rigid in his strict adherence to the teachings of Scripture, but it was from this very intolerance for sin and compromise that the profound ministry of Robert Lewis Dabney drew its strength.

His Views

Like all men—even great prophets—Dabney had his shortcomings. No doubt some will point to these and miss the significance of his message. Others will simply object to his strong advocacy of the Southern cause. I would urge those readers to suspend judgement until they have had the opportunity to more carefully study his writings and the context of the War itself. Still others may shy away from the strong opinions and unequivocal language interspersed with humor which was Dabney's trademark. It would be a mistake to attempt to evaluate his writings through the clouded lenses of modernity which shuns strong men of conviction. However, for those individuals who long for the days in which a gentleman could hold the door for a lady without some indignant feminist snorting at him, Dabney's writings will seem refreshingly virile. Even this virility may give discomfort to those modern examples of the male sex whose very vocabulary is littered with the terminology of post-feminist America. One must not forget that Dabney wrote in the last great period of American history in which men were proud to be men, and to call someone a "patriarch" was to pay him a compliment.

This booklet reveals the late, great theologian through some of his more interesting maxims, quips and prophetic declarations. It is by no means exhaustive. You have before you just a few morsels of interest from the table of this prolific author. The quotes taken from a variety of his

Introduction

writings have been divided into four subjects: The Family; Education; Politics; and Feminism. I have selected quotes on these topics because of the lasting importance and current relevance of the subject matter.

As to his predictions, the reader must remember that Dabney was simply stating what appeared perfectly obvious to him. For example, long before the birth of the modern home schooling movement, Dabney praised home-based training as the superior method for the education of children. Long before universal compulsory education, Dabney accurately predicted that the creation of a mandatory system of government-funded education would lead to a higher crime rate and lower academic standards.

In a sense, Dabney predicted the recent brouhaha of Goals 2000 and Outcome Based Education (OBE) when he declared that government education would inevitably lead to an unholy alliance between unions interested in power, textbook manufacturers desirous of a monopoly share of the industry at taxpayer expense, and special interest groups hoping to foist their intellectual anarchy on the children of the nation. He explained that government money always brought government control, but predicted that many Christians would quickly trade their freedom for state money, and ultimately lose both.

Dabney decried the attempts of those individuals who hoped to sanitize the government schools with classroom prayer. Who would pray? To whom would the prayers be directed—a god that appeals to the lowest common denominator of pluralistic sentiment? Dabney recognized what most modern Evangelicals fail to comprehend, namely, that even the best prayers can not make acceptable a system that is inherently wrong. The ultimate problem with government schools would be that they exist. Either such schools would be Christian, or they would be anti-Christian, with no accommodating middle ground. And by what right, Dabney argued, did the State demand the right to educate children, an inescapably religious task? Because the state is both incapable and unsuited for the propagation of Christian education, any attempt to establish such a system would ultimately result in an affront to Gospel Christianity. Can the reader deny that each of Dabney's predictions have come true? The classrooms of our nation have become crime zones, the literacy rates of our students have fallen to appalling lows, and our children in government schools are daily indoctrinated in the religion of Humanism.

His choicest words were reserved for the feminists of his day; the suffragettes. He accurately predicted that the women's rights movement would lead to the emasculation of men, the end of the nuclear family and the overthrow of Western culture. He joked that the feminists would not be satisfied until ladies wore pants, played sports with men, grew beards and sang bass—at least 50% of which has come to pass. Dabney proclaimed that there was a direct link between the rabid egalitarian spirit of the women's rights movement and similar anti-authoritarian movements. In fact, he argued that the push for women's rights would ultimately lead to a similar push for the emancipation of children from the oppression of the family. Dabney never read the United Nations Convention on the Rigths of the Child, but he certainly anticipated many of its key tenets.

If we are to accept Dabney's logic as valid, we are then left with the inescapapble conclusion that much of the political efforts advanced by many Evangelicals are ill-conceived, misguided and doomed to failure. If Dabney was correct, then even if efforts to put prayer back into government schools were successful, the results would do little more than place a Band-Aid on a malignant cancer. If Dabney was correct, then the frantic push for vouchers by Christian conservatives is yet another move toward socialism, wealth redistribution, the state establishment of religion, and government control over the private sector. If Dabney was correct, we will continue to see crime and illiteracy rise in direct proportion to the growth of tax-payer subsidized education.

Dabney's Legacy

The legacy of Robert Lewis Dabney is that of a man who "understood the times." An able historian, he not only predicted with devastating accuracy the end result of the compromises of his day, but because he knew the past, he had a sense of the magnitude of what was being lost. As you read these few selected quotes from the writings of this prolific author, keep in mind that the genius of Robert Lewis Dabney is found in his ability to comprehend the lessons of history in light of the eternal truths of Scripture, and, having done so, to apply those principles to the constantly changing circumstances of the time in which God had placed him.

Thus, Dabney not only predicts the future, but he reminds us of our past. Of course, Americans are notorious for our ability to play Monday morning quarterback. We enjoy pontificating about the obvious mistakes of those men who walked before we did. We are confident that were we in their place, the mistake would have been avoided. After all, how could they have been so blind, so half-hearted, so compromising? We think to ourselves: If only this general had not retreated, he would have seized the day; If only this one good politician had remained true to his oath of office, the freedom of a nation would be secure; If only this preacher had not allowed the little compromises, his children would not have rebelled; If only this man had mustered the courage to say "no" to small sins when he was a boy, he would not be behind bars today.

And, while sitting in the comfort of our homes, televisions on, with our bellies full of food and heads full of frivolity and froth, glibly pronouncing judgement on the past, we are oblivious to the oblivious, namely, that we, too, stand on the precipice of destruction facing the same questions as the men we criticize, only in different circumstances. Will we answer differently? Most will not. Hence, the tragedy of history: God has given the answers to the problems, he has shown us the consequences, and yet most will not listen, because they choose not to listen. That is why, lurking in the background, ever conscious of mankind's ability to forget the most fundamental lessons of history, the well-worn adage cries to all who will listen and act: "He who forgets the past is condemned to repeat it!"

Blaise Pascal once wrote that when everyone is heading with a rapid pace for destruction, the individual who simply stops will stick out like a fixed point. Robert Lewis Dabney was such a point. May God give us more men like him.

Douglas W. Phillips
January, 1997
Leesburg, Virginia

❦ I ❦

Dabney on Education

On How State Education Money Can Corrupt Good People

Imperial Donatives to the Roman populace became very popular; true, but they poisoned the last good element of Roman character, and helped to complete the putrescence of the empire. I fear it is only too true, that this cunning cheat of Yankee state-craft is alluring the poor, harassed Southern parent; and that he is yeilding to the bait which promises deceitfully to relieve him of his parental responsibility....A bribe, alas, may become easily popular in decadent times.

Just Because the Idea is New Does Not Make It Better

Young people think old folks are fools, but old people know that young ones are. Did that old system produce perfect results? No. No system in imperfect human hands ever produces perfect results. Did it teach every adult in the state to read and write? No. But neither will the new one....And after all the fuss and inquitous expense, "the upshot" will be that there will still be just as many adults in the state, who practically will not read, and who will forget how as before. And there will be far fewer to use the art of reading to any good purpose.

The Evidence Indicates That Government Education is a Flop

My prediction is already verified in Massachusetts, the very home of the state-school humbug. The annual reports of their own school superintendents confess it. A large part of the rural laboring population still do not read, have forgotten how to read, do not care to know, and care not a sliver whether their own children know. (Here by the way is the cause of this new furor over compulsory education.) Tried by this sober and truthful standard, I assert that the comparative fruit of the old system will fully justify its excellence. Again I demand that the tree will be known by its fruits.

Parents Must Privately Control Education

Instead of the State undertaking to be universal creator and sustainer of schools, let it invite parents to create, sustain and govern their own schools under the assitence and guidance of an inexperienced and unsalaried board.

The Pagan Presupposition Behind Compulsory Education

It is the teaching of the Bible and of sound political ethics that the education of children belongs to the sphere of the family and is the duty of the parents. The theory that children of the commonwealth are the charge of the commonwealth is a pagan one derived from heathen Sparta and Plato's heathen republic, and connected by regular, logical sequence with legalized prostitution and the dissolution of the conjugal tie.

Parents vs. The State

The parents are the real architects of their children's destiny, and the state cannot help it.

Government Education Will Lead to an Increase in Juvenile Crime

They say: "It costs less money to build schoolhouses than jails." But what if it turns out that the state's expenditure is one of the things which necessitates the expenditure in jails?

Government Education Has a Poor Track Record

The northern states of the union had previously to the war all adopted the system of universal state schools, and the southern states had not. In 1850, the former had thirteen and a half millions of people, and twenty three thousand six hundred and sixty four (23,664) criminal convictions. The South (without state schools) had nine and a half millions, and two thousand nine hundred and twenty one (2,921) criminal convictions—that is to say, after allowing for the difference in population, the "educated" masses were something more than six times more criminal as the "uneducated." That same year, the North was supporting 114,00 paupers and the South 20,500. The "unintelligent" South was something more than four times as well qualified to provide for its own substistence than the "intelligent North"! But Massachusetts is the native home of the public school in America...In the South, state schoolhouses were unknow, and consequently jails and penitentiaries were on the most confined and humble scale. The North is studded over with grand and costly public schoolhouses and her jails are even more palatial in extent and more numerous than they.

Home Education is the Key to Success

The home education has so much more potential than that of the school, that the little modicum of training which a common school system can give to the average masses is utterly trivial and impotent as a means of reversing the child's tendency.

Compulsory and Free Education: That Which Costs Nothing is Never Valued

There is a natural humiliation in being compelled to accept the provision of charity, or of the state, for that which conscience tells parents is obligatory on them. These reasons account for the fact, which the advocates of public schools so desire to hide, that the children do not attend, and the parents do not care to make them attend...The rising movement for compulsory education is a confession of this fact.

On the Means of Charity

The agency must be social and Christian. The work must be done by laying hold of the sentiments, hearts, and consciences of parents and children together—not through their grammatical and arithmetical faculties. The agents for this blessed work are the neighbor and the church. Christian charity and zeal, with the potent social influences descending from superiors to inferiors in a society which is practically a kindly and liberal aristocracy; these may break the reign of ignorance and unaspiring apathy. The state cannot; the work is above its sphere.

Dabney Opposes Bible Reading in Government Schools Because He Opposes Government Schools

The absolute necessity of Bible instruction in schools is then argued with irresistible force. Yet with all this, such is the difficulty which we are pressing, it betrays this able writer into saying: "I do not propose to allude to the agitating question of the introduction of the Scriptures into public schools conducted under authority of government." But why not? If other schools so imperatively need this element of Bible instruction, why do not the state schools? Its necessity is argued from principle which are of universal application to beigns who have souls. Why shall not the application be made to all schools? Alas! The answer is: the right conclusion cannot be applied to state schools. We claim, then, this is a complete demonstration that the state is unfit to assume the educational function. The argument is as plain and perfect as any that can be imagined. Here is one part which is absolutely essential to the work of right eduction: the state is effectively disabled from performing that part. Then the state cannot educate and should not profess it. The argument is parallel to this: in order to be a country physician, it is essential that one should ride in all weathers. Mr. A cannot ride in bad weather. Then Mr. A cannot be a country physician. And if he is an honest man, he will not profess to be.

Only Christian Education is True Education

Tuition in Christianity is essential to all education which is worth the name. And we claim more than the admission that each man should at some stage of his training and by somebody by taught Christianity; we mean in the fullest sense that Christianity must be a present element of all training at all times or else it is not true and valuable education.

The moral judgments and acts of the soul all involve an exercise of reason, so that it is impossible to separate the ethical and intellectual functions…Man fulfills the ends of his existence, not by right cognitions, but by right moral actions…The nature of responsibility is such that there can be no neutrality between duty and sin. He that is not with his God is against Him…Hence, as there cannot be in any soul a non-Christian state which is not anti-Christian, it follows that any training which attempts to be non-Christian is therefore anti-Christian…How obvious then that a let-alone policy as to the moral development must to a greater of lesser degree amount to a positive development of vicious character? Not to row, is itself, to float down the stream. Should the branches and leaves of a tree continue to grow while the roots remain stationary (i.e. the same size), it would result in the destruction of the tree, and this, although the roots contracted no positive disease or weakness. The first gale would blow it over in consequence of the disroportion of its parts.

To educate the mind without purifying the heart is but to place a sharp sword in the hands of a madman.

There can be, therefore, no true education without moral culture, and no true moral culture without Christianity. The very power of the teacher in the schoolroom is either moral or it is a degrading brute force. But he can show the child no other moral basis for it but the Bible. Hence my argument is as perfect as clear, the teacher must be

Christian. But the American commonwealth has promised to have no religious character. Then it cannot be teacher. If it undertakes to be, it must be consistent, and go on and unite church and state. Are you ready to follow your opinions to this consistent end?

That Some Survive Government Schools is No Justification for Others Taking the Same Course

Someone might say that this broad proposition is refuted at the outset by frequent instances of persons who received, at least during a part of their youth, a training perfectly non-Christian, and who yet are very useful, and even Christian citizens. The answer is yes: It is the prerogative of a merciful Providence, and the duty of His children to repair the defects and misfortunes of His creatures and to bring good out of evil. But surely this comes far short of a justification for us if we willingly employ faulty methods which have a regular tendency to work evil. Surely it is not our privilege to make mischief for God and good Christians to repair!

On How Public Education Will Lead to Woe

(This) "nostrum" of free school education, (has been) in full force, for two generations...Did not this very system rear us that very generation, which in its blind ignorance and brutal passion, has recently wrecked the institutions of America, has filled our country with destitution, woe and murder; and, with a stupid blindness, only equaled by its wickedness, has stripped its own Commonwealths, in order to wreak its mad spite on ours, of the whole safeguards for their own freedom and peace? These are the true fruits of this...system of state primary education.

Dabney On Compulsion and Redistribution of Wealth

Your "free schools" like not a few of the other pretensions of radicalism are in fact exactly opposite to the name falsely assumed. The great bulk of those who pay the money for them do it, not freely, but by compulsion. They are virtually thrust down our throats by the bayonet, and the exemplars you most boast and imitate, not only make the payment compulsory, but the attendance also, as your consistency will doubtless cause you to do in Virginia also in a few years. The only freedom of your system is your freedom to compel other people's money.

Notwithstanding your glorying then, I mean once more to assert the unfashionable truth. Truth is never out of date. It has sometimes happened that a tentative experience has thrown so much light upon a bad system as to reopen the discussion with better guidance than the previous.

Dabney Assails Pro-Government-School Protestant Hypocrites

Note: Dabney points out 1) that America is a society made up of diverse religions; 2) that our form of government will not tolerate the establishment of one sect over another; 3) that violent riots, protests, and hand to hand combat have broken out because certain non-Protestants have objected to the use of the King James Bible in the common schools, and 4) that the same principle which leads Protestants to object to having their tax money go to subsidized Roman Catholic education should lead Protestants to respect the rights of Catholics not to be coerced into subsidizing Protestant education. The most numerous and determined complaints are, of course, Roman Catholics, but the Jews are now becoming increasingly more numerous and influential, and the Unitarians and Deists must claim similar grounds of protest. The argument is that this version of Scripture is, in their sincere judgment, erroneous; and therefore, they cannot conscientiously permit it to be taught to their children. But as they are taxed to support their schools, they cannot be justly perverted to teach their children an obnoxious creed without a virtual establishment of the Protestant religion at public expense; which is an outrage against the fundamental principles and laws of the state.

We have covenanted that in our political relations as citizens of the common wealth, all shall have equal rights irrespective of their religion. In that sphere, we are bound to be impartial, our word is out. The very point of the covenant is, that so far as civic rights and privileges go, our Romanist fellow citizens' opinions (erroneous though we may deem them in our religious judgment) shall be respected precisely as they are required to respect ours. The weight of the Romanist protest, then, cannot be consistently evaded by American republicans.

Dabney Sees Only Three Viable Alternatives for State Education

1) One is to force the religion of the majority on the children of the minority of the people.

2) A second solution is what the British call the "plan of concurrent endowment." It consists in aiding the citizens of different religions to gather their children in separate schools, in which religious instruction may be given suited to the views of the parents and all paid for by the state alike… It outrages the rights of Protestants by expending part of the money they pay to propagate opinions which they regard as false and destructive, and it gives to erroneous creeds a

pecuniary and moral support beyond that which they draw from the zeal and free gifts of their own votaries.

3) The third alternative propose is to limit the teaching of the state schools in every case to secular learning, leaving the parents to supply such religious instruction as they se fit in their own way and time, or to neglect it wholly. Of this solution no Christian of any name can be an advocate. We have seen how utterly the Pope and his prelates reprobate it. All other denominations in Europe regard it as monstrous; and indeed no adherent of any religion can be found in any other age or country than America who would not pronounce it wicked and absurd for any agency undertaking the education of youth to leave the religious culture an absolute blank. Testimonies might be sighted to weariness.

Moral Education is Impossible Without Jesus Christ

In an annual meeting of the Teacher's Association of the State of Maryland, a well considered piece was read by a prominent member, in which the immense difficulty of the religious questions in State schools was fairly displayed. The author, on the other hand, admitted that the rights of conscience of parents could not be justly disregarded. He held, on the other hand , that a schooling devoid of moral and religious teaching ought to be utterly inadmissible. The best solution he could suggest was that the State should get up a course if moral and theological dogmas for its pupils, embracing only those common truths in which all parties are agreed, and excluding every truth to which any one party took exception. And he admitted that, as we have Protestants, Papists, Unitarians, Jews, Deists, etc. (not to say Mormons and the heathen Chinese), the Bible and all its characteristic doctrines must be excluded! It is too plain that when the State school's creed had been pruned of every proposition to which any one party objected, it would be worthless and odious in the eyes of every party, and would be too emasculated to do any child's soul a particle of good.

The Common Schools Educate for Sloth, Not for Usefulness

The use of letters is not education, but only one means of education, and not the only means. The laboring classes find their appropriate mental and moral cultivation in their tasks themselves and in the example and influence of the superiors for whom they labor. The plowman or artisan cultivates his mental faculties most appropriately in acquiring skill and resource for his work. He trains his moral virtues by the fidelity and endurance with which he performs that work. He ennobles his taste and sentiments by looking up to the superior who employs him. If to these influences you add the awakening, elevating, expanding force of Christian principles, you have given the laborer a true education—a hundredfold more true, more suitable, more useful, than the communication of certain literary arts, which he will almost necessarily disuse. Let the reader recall the brilliant passage of Macaulay...that the Athenian populous, without books, was a highly cultivated people. Let him remember how entirely the greatness of the feudal barons in the Middle Ages dissociated from all "clerky arts;" yet they were warriors, statesmen, poets, and gentlemen.

Dabney Opposes using Children as Missionaries in Government Schools

Sometimes it is asked, "How are the degraded classes to be elevated if they are thus to be denied all associations with those better than themselves?" We reply that while we fully recognize the Christian duty of seeking the degraded and of drawing them up to purer associations, we beg leave to demur against employing our innocent and inexperienced children as the missionaries. The braving of this moral contagion is the proper work of mature men and women of virtue; and these are to elevate their beneficiaries b holding to them the relation of benevolent superiors, not of comrades and equals in schoolroom and playground.

Evil Peer-Grouping is Inherent in the Government School Classroom

It is claimed that it is the teacher's part to prevent those "evil communications which corrupt good manners." We reply that it is impossible; he would need more than the hundred hands of Briareus and the hundred eyes of Argus, with more moral fidelity than falls to the share of any save apostles and martyrs. Is the pittance paid to a common school teacher likely to purchase all these splendid endowments?

The Church Does Not Have Jurisdiction to Be the Primary Educator of Children

The Church's duty is to instruct parents on how God would have them rear their children, and enforce the duty by spiritual sanction; but there its official power ends. It does not usurp the doing of the important task it inculcates.

If the State Educates, the Education will be Manipulated by Partisan Interets

Now, let...the state become the educator, and there is just the same risk that the education of the youth will be perverted to subserve a faction, and that, by the hateful means of imbuing their minds with error and passion in place of truth and right. The result is despotism of a party instead of a pope. One may be as bad as the other.

The Public School Teacher is the Agent of the State

The state school teacher is her [i.e., the state's] official and teaches by her authority. All school officials derive their authority from State laws, hence all their functions are as truly state actions as those of the sheriff in hanging, or the judge in sentencing a murder.

Education Can Not be Neutral

If secular education is to be made consistently and honestly non-Christian, then...they must submit to a mutilation and falsification far worse than absolute omission. It is hard to conceive how a teacher is to keep his covenant faithfully with the State so as to teach history, cosmogony, psychology, ethics, the laws of nations as to insinuate nothing favorable or unfavorable touching the preferred beliefs of either evangelical Christians, Papists, Socinians, Deists, pantheists, Materialists or Fetish worshipers who claim equal rights.

❦ II ❦

Dabney on Politics

On Biblical Voting Ethics and Against Slavish Partisan Loyalties

We would say, with all the earnestness and emphasis which the most solemn feeling can inspire, let each individual Christian in our land,—whether he sits in our halls of legislature, or rules as a magistrate, or guides public opinion through the press, or merely fills the station of the private citizen—consider his own personal concern in this matter. We would affectionately individualize each man and say to him, "My brother, thou art the man. Consider what would God have you do?" Every Christian man, whether lawmaker or law executor or voter, should carry his Christian conscience, enlightened by God's word, into his political duty in another manner than we have been accustomed to do. We must ask less what party caucuses and leaders dictate, and more what duty dictates; for the day is at hand when we shall be brought to an awful judgment for the thoughtless manner in which we exercise our civic function.

My brethren, the Christians of this land are able to control the selection of reckless and wicked men for the places of trust, if they please, and will do their duty. Here are four millions of men and women, chiefly adults, among a people of twenty-six millions…

four millions who profess to be supremely ruled by principles of righteousness, peace and love, and to be united to each other in the brotherhood of a heavenly birth. If even the voters among these would go together to the polls to uphold the cause of peace, they would turn the scale of every election.

How often have we gone on Monday to the hustings [i.e., the political arena], after having appeared on Sabbath as the servants of the Price of Peace and brethren of all his servants, and, in our political heats, speedily forgotten that we were Christians? Let each Christian citizen have his independent political predilections, and support them with decision, if you please. Let them, if need be, render that enlightened and moderate allegiance to the party of their choice which is supposed to be essential in free governments. But when their party demands of them that they shall sustain men of corrupt private morals or reckless passions, because of their supposed party orthodoxy, let all Christians say: "Nay, verily, we would feign yield all reasonable party fidelity; but we are also partisans in the commonwealth of King Jesus, and our allegiance to Him transcends all others. Unless you will present to us a man who to party orthodoxy unites private virtues, we can not sustain him." Then would their reasonable demand be potential in every party, and the abuse would be crushed. And this stand, if taken by Christian citizens, we affirm, would infringe no personal or associated rights; for is there any party who would admit that it had not a single member respectable, virtuous, and sober enough to deserve the suffrages of Christian political competition and hide itself in oblivion!

Christians will be Judged by God if They Vote for the Unjust

When you elevate a bad man, you give to him a hundred-fold more power of example to corrupt your sons, and your neighbor's sons by his evil acts. Those acts are a hundred-fold more conspicuous and more weighty to attract notice and imitation than if you had left him in his deserved obscurity. When you delegate your money, influence or civic power to a bad man, you make his wicked official acts and influences your own; he is your chosen agent, and acts for you, and be assured a jealous God will not forget to visit the people for the guilt thus contracted.

Do Not Vote for Those who will Unjustly Send Your Sons to War

And when the rash representatives in our halls of legislation and our newspapers shall have sown the wind, who will reap the whirlwind? When they have scattered the dragon's teeth, who must meet that horrent crop which they will produce? Not they alone, but you, your sons, your friends and their sons. So that these misleaders of the people, while you so weakly connive at their indiscretions, may indirectly be preparing the weapon which is to pierce the bosom of your fair-haired boy, and summoning the birds of prey, which are to pick out those eyes whose joy is now the light of your happy homes. For your own sakes, for your children's sakes, arise, declare that from this day no money, no vote, no influence of yours shall go to the maintenance of any other counsels than those of moderation, righteousness and manly forbearance.

Partisan Politics and Political Compromise

It may be inferred again that the present movement for women's rights will certainly prevail from the history of its only opponent, Northern conservatism. This is a party which never conserves anything. Its history has been that is demurs to each aggression of the progressive party, and aims to save its credit by a respectable amount of growling, but always acquiesces at last in the innovation. What was the resisted novelty of yesterday is today one of the accepted principles of conservatism; it is now conservative only in affecting to resist the next innovation, which will tomorrow be forced upon its timidity and will be succeeded by some third revolution, to be denounced and then adopted in its turn. American conservatism is merely the shadow that follows Radicalism as it moves forward towards perdition. It remains behind it, but never retards it, and always advances near its leader. This pretended salt hath utterly lost its savor: wherewith shall it be salted? Its impotency is not hard, indeed, top explain. It is worthless because it is the conservatism of expediency only, and not of sturdy principle. It intends to risk nothing serious for the sake of the truth, and has no idea of being guilty of the folly of martyrdom. It always—when about to enter a protest—very blandly informs the wild beast whose path it essays to stop, that its "bark is worse that its bite," and that it only means to save its manners by enacting its decent role of resistance. The only practical purpose which it now subserves in American politics is to give enough exercise to Radicalism to keep it "in wind," and to prevent its becoming pursy and lazy from having nothing to whip. No doubt, after a few years, when women's suffrage shall have become an accomplished fact, conservatism will tacitly admit it into its creed, and thenceforward plume itself upon its wise firmness in opposing with similar weapons the extreme of baby suffrage; and when that too shall have been won, it will be heard declaring that the integrity of the American Constitution requires at least the refusal of suffrage to asses. There it will assume, with great dignity, its final position.

Compromise

In this day innovations march with rapid strides. The fantastic suggestions of yesterday, entertained only by a few fanatics, and then only mentioned by the sober to be ridiculed, is today the audacious reform, and will be tomorrow the recognized usage. Novelties are so numerous and so wild and rash, that even in conservative minds the sensibility of wonder is exhausted and the instinct of righteous resistance fatigued.

The Bible, Not Human Experience, is the Final Authority

Modern society, while condemning sternly many things which the ancients tolerated or even applauded, countenances some things which they utterly rejected. It is very pleasant and natural for us to quietly assume that ours if the advanced and civilized age. But when men reason thus, "A given usage cannot be improper, because Christian opinion and society allow it among us," they reason in a circle. If the propriety of the usage is in questions, then there are two hypotheses to be examined, of which one is, "Ours is a pure state, and therefore what we tolerate must be pure;" but the other is, "This tolerated usage being impure, it proves our state corrupt." Now, the decision between the two hypotheses cannot be made by a self-sufficient assumption. Oriental, Greek and Papal Christianity ((***justifies***)) (should be "justify"???) many things which we think excessive corruptions by just such an assumption. It is no more valid in our case than in theirs. Indeed, the very tendency to such self-sufficiency is, according to the Bible, one of the strongest symptoms of corruption. The matter must be settled by a fair appeal to Bible morals.

Republican Government, Not Democracy, Favored by God

While the Bible history does not prohibit stronger forms of government per se, it indicates God's preference for the representative republic as distinguished from the leveling democracy; and to this theory of human rights all its moral teachings correspond. On the other hand, it constitutes civil society of superiors, inferiors and equals (see Shorter Catechism, Question 64), making the household represented by the parent and master the integral unit of the social fabric, assigning to each order, higher or lower, its rule or subordination under the distributive equity of the law. On the other hand, it protects each order in its legal privileges, and prohibits oppression and injustice as to all.

❦ III ❦

Dabney on the Family

A Revival of Fatherhood and Parental Responsibility

The religious importance of parental obligation may be inferred from many scriptural truths; and, among others, from the place it occupies at the end of the old dispensation and the beginning of the new. Historians tell us that from the prophesying o Malachi to the Christian era was an interval of more than four hundred years. During all these ages the heavens were silent, and the church received oracle neither by "Urim and Thummim," nor by prophetic voice. Malachi, in his last chapter, prepares the people for this long silence of revelation by two works, of which one is a promise, and the other a precept. The command is (chap. 4:4) to walk by the law of Moses, God's servant, and to keep the statutes and judgments given, through hum, for all Israel. The promise is, that in due time the Messiah's forerunner, coming in the spirit and power of Elijah, shall usher in the solemn, yet glorious day of Christ, by preparatory ministry. This was to be, therefore, the next prophet whom the church was entitled to expect. But his work was to be prominently a revival of parental fidelity and domestic piety. "He shall turn the heart of the father to the children, and the hear of the children to their fathers, lest I come and smite the earth with a curse."

The next recorded message from the skies is that of the Angel Gabriel to Zacharias, given in Luke 1:11-20. The heavenly herald begins just where the earthly prophet had ended, with the promise and work of the forerunner, who was to be Zacharias's son. "And he shall go before him (the Lord) in the spirit and power of Elijah, to turn the hearts of the fathers to the children, and the disobedient to the wisdom of the just, to make ready a people prepared for the Lord" (v.17). That this work upon fathers and children was to be far more than the removal of domestic alienations; that is was to include this, but also to embrace a great revival of parental and filial piety, an awakening of the parents' hearts to the salvation of their children, and the docile seeking and reception of parental instruction by the children,—this is plain from the whole passage; it is a turning of both to God, and a "turning of the disobedient to the wisdom of the just." We are reminded also [that] our Savior told his people that, oftentimes, his gospel was the occasion, though an innocent one, of family alienation, rather than reconciliations. Luke 7:51: "Suppose ye that I am come to give peace on earth: I tell you, Nay but rather division."

This revival of domestic piety and parental fidelity to the soul of children, Malachi declares, is necessary to prevent the coming of the Divine Messiah from being a woe, instead of a blessing, to men. This reform alone prevents his coming to "smite the land with a curse," instead of crowning it with mercies; because the wickedness, which would otherwise prevail among men, would outrage the holiness instead of attracting the compassion of the incarnate God. According to the angel, the same reform is the appointed means to "make ready a people prepared for the Lord: ((Should have end quote before colon?)) God's way of promoting revival, then, is not to increase the activity of any public and outward means only, but "to turn the hearts of the parents to the children."

This review shows us also that the duty of parental fidelity is equally prominent in both dispensations. The old terminates with it; the new opens with it. This is the connecting link between both; it is the hinge in which they meet and combine with each other. How plain it is that God regards it as of prime practical importance for man's salvation!

The Awe of Parenthood

It is enough for us jut to know that God, by his mysterious works of creation and providence, does empower human parents for this amazing result—the origination, out of nothing, of a new being—and that a rational, immortal spirit. How solemn, how high, this prerogative! It raises man nearer the almighty Creator, in his supreme prerogative as Master of all things, than anything else that is done by creatures on earth or in heaven. Angels are not thus endued. The responsibility of this relation is not fully seen by merely regarding the infant as a beautiful animal, organized, in miniature, after the kind of the parents. It is the mysterious propagation of a rational soul that fills the reflecting mind with awe. The parent looks upon the tender face which answers to his caress with an infantile smile; he should see beneath that smile an immoral spark which he has kindled, but can never quench. It must grow, for weal or for woe; it cannot be arrested. Just now it was not/ The parents have mysteriously brought it from darkness and nothing. There is no power beneath God's throne that can remand it back to nothing, should existence prove a curse. Yes; the parents have lighted there an everlasting lamp, which must burn on when the sun shall have been turned into darkness and the moon into blood, either with the glory of heaven or the lurid flame of despair.

The Necessity of Parental Instruction

Now, it is fully admitted that neither divine nor human law gives a parent the right to force the tender mind of the child by persecutions of corporeal pains or penalties; or to abuse it, by sophistries or falsehoods, in to the adoption of his opinions. But this power the providential law does confer; the parent may and ought to avail himself of all the influences of opportunity and example, of filial reverence and affection, of his superior age, knowledge, and sagacity, to reinforce the power of truth over the child's mind, and, in this good sense, to prejudice him in favor of the parental creed. And how potent is this influence! Does is not almost commit the spiritual liberty of the young to a human hand? How mighty the power of opportunity which the parent is thus authorized to employ to propagate his creed on another—while as yet the pupil is ignorant of the process wrought upon him, and incapable of resisting it! There is no power beneath the skies, authorized by God, that is so far-reaching, so near the prerogatives of God himself; and for the reason there is none so solemnly responsible. When God has clothed you, O parent! with such powers, with results so beneficent and glorious, and has thus made you so nearly a god to your own children, do you suppose that you can neglect or pervert them without being held to a dire account? It were better for that man that a millstone were hanged about his neck, and that he were drowned in the depths of the sea. Here appears a new argument to prove man's responsibility for his moral and religious opinions. The code which he heartily believes is, to him, his authoritative creed. It is to this the privilege of parental inculcation must practically apply. Hence, he who has perverted his own reason and conscience to mistake a lie for the truth, makes himself responsible, not only for his own destruction, but for the probable destruction of the children. God has submitted to his guidance. Take heed, then parents, how you hear and how you believe, not only for your own sakes but for your children's sakes.

Parental Love is Foundational to a Free Society

But what does the maker of our frames mean by planting and preserving thin master affection in human hearts? It tells us, in accents as sweet as they are potent, the duty which parents owe to children, and children to their parents. It is God's teaching in the inmost heart, instructing us that the fulfillment of this affection is the highest, holiest, most urgent of all the earthly duties man owes. Parental love is the main bond ((or)) (should be "of"???)) human society among creatures otherwise selfish and unjust as fallen men are. Without it society would doubtless degenerate into anarchy and men into savages. Can any reasonable mind believe, then, that God will overlook this manner of affection in his plans for the sanctification of a fallen work, or that God's true grace can be prevalent in any parent's heart, an not energize and direct this love?

IV

Dabney on Feminism & Biblical Manhood

Women Preachers

A few years ago the public preaching of women was universally condemned among all conservative denominations of Christians, and, indeed, within their bounds, was entirely unknown. Now the innovation is brought face to face even with the Southern churches and female preachers are knocking at our doors. We are told that already public opinion is so truckling before the boldness and plausibility of their claims that ministers of our own communions begin to hesitate, and men hardly know whether they have the moral courage to adhere to the right.

The Rise of Feminism

In our day, innovations march with so rapid a stride that they quite take away one's breath. The fantastical project of yesterday, which was mentioned only to be ridiculed, is today the audacious reform, and will be tomorrow the accomplished fact. Such has been the history of the agitation for "women's rights," as they are sophistically called in this country. A few years ago this movement was the especial hobby of a few old women of both sexes, who made themselves the laughing-stock of all sane people by the annual ventilation of their crotchet. Their only recruits were a few of the unfortunates whom nature or fortune had debarred from those triumphs and enjoyments which are the natural ambition of the sex, and who adopted this agitation as the most feasible mode of expressing their spitefulness against the successful competitors. Today the movement has assumed such dimensions that it challenges the attention of every thoughtful mind.

Paul Was Not a Male Chauvinist

How many thousands of women are there, professed members of Christ's church, who rid themselves of all these [biblical] precepts with a disdainful toss, saying: "Oh! Paul was but a crusty bachelor. It was the men who legislated thus in their pride of sex. Had women written, all would have been different." I would request such fair reasoners to look this question steadily in the face. Is this the legislation of men, or of God speaking by men? If they say the former, is not this virtual infidelity? If the latter, had they not better take care, "lest haply they be found even fighting against God," instead of against a "crusty old bachelor"?

Cultural Androgyny

If we understand the claims of the Women's Rights women, they are in substance two: 1) that the legislation, at least, of society shall disregard all the natural distinctions of the sexes, and award the same specific rights and franchises to both in every respect; and 2) that woman while in the married state shall be released from every species of conjugal subordination. The assimilation of the garments of the two sexes, their competition in the same industries and professions, and their common access to the same amusements and recreations, are social changes which the "strong-minded" expect to work, each one for herself, when once the obstructions of law are removed from other points.

The Devastating Consequences of Feminism

So it will be found (and it is no disparagement to woman to say it) that the very traits which fit her to be the angel of a virtuous home unfit her to meet the agitations of political life, even as safely as does the more rugged man. The hot glare of publicity and passion will speedily deflower her delicacy and sweetness. Those temptations, which her Maker did not form her to bear, will debauch her heart, developing a character as much more repulsive than that of the debauched man as the fall has been greater. The politicating woman, unsexed and denaturalized, shorn of the true glory of her femininity, will appear to men as a feeble hybrid mannikin [dwarf], with all the defects and none of the strength of the male. Instead of being the dear object of his chivalrous affection, she becomes his importunate rival, despised without being feared.

Women's Rights Will Lead to the Abolition of Marriage

This suggests a third consequence, which some of the advocates of the movement even already are bold enough to foreshadow. "Women's Rights" means the abolition of all permanent marriage ties. We are told that Mrs. Cady Stanton avowed this result, proclaiming it at the invitation of the Young Men's Christian Association of New York. She holds that woman's bondage is not truly dissolved until the marriage bond is annulled. She is thoroughly consistent. Some hoodwinked advocates of her revolution may be blind to the sequence; but it is inevitable. It must follow by this cause, if for no other, that the unsexed politicating woman can never inspire in man that true affection on which marriage should be founded. Men will doubtless be still sensual; but it is simply impossible that they can desire them for the pure and sacred sphere of the wife. Let every woman ask herself: will she choose for the lord of her affections an unsexed effeminate man? No more can man be drawn to the masculine woman. The mutual attraction of the two complementary halves is gone forever.

The abolition of marriage would follow again by another cause. The divergent interests and the rival independence of the two equal wills would be irreconcilable with domestic government, or union, or peace. Shall the children of this monstrous no-union be held responsible to two variant coordinate and supreme wills at once? Heaven pity the children! Shall the two parties to this perpetual co-partnership have neither the power to secure the performance of the mutual duties nor to dissolve it? It is a self-contradiction, an impossible absurdity. Such a co-partnership of equals with independent interests must be separable at will, as all other such co-partnerships are. The only relation between the sexes which will remain will be a cohabitation continuing so long as the convenience or caprice of both parties may suggest; and this, with most, will amount to a vagrant concubinage.

The Character of the Children of Feminists

What will be the character of the children reared under such a domestic organization as this? If human experience has established anything at all, it is the truth of that principle announced by the Hebrew prophet when he declared that the great aim of God in ordaining a permanent tie between one man and one woman was "that

He might seek a godly seed." God's ordinance, the only effective human ordinance for checking and curbing the first tendencies to evil, is domestic, parental government. When the family shall no longer have a head, and the great foundation for the subordination of children—the mother's example—is gone; when the mother shall have found another sphere than her home for her energies; when she shall have exchanged the sweet charities of domestic love and sympathy for the fierce passions of the hustings [i.e., the political arena]; when families shall be disrupted at the caprice of either party, and the children scattered as foundlings from their hearthstone,—it requires no wisdom to see that a race of sons will be reared nearer akin to devils than to men. In the hands of such a bastard progeny, without discipline, without homes, without a God, the last remains of social order will speedily perish, and society will be overwhelmed in savage anarchy.

Feminism is an Attack Against Femininity

It would not be hard to show, did space permit, that this movement on the part of these women is as suicidal as it is mischievous. Its certain result will be the re-enslavement of women, not under the Scriptural bonds of marriage, but under the yoke of literal corporeal force.

The woman who will calmly review the condition of her sex in other ages and countries will feel that her wisdom is to "let will enough alone." Physically, the female is the "weaker vessel." This world is a hard and selfish scene where the weaker goes to the wall. Under all other civilizations and all other religions than ours woman has experienced this fate to the full; her condition has been that of a slave to the male—sometimes a petted slave, but yet a slave.

In Christian and European society alone has she ever attained the place of man's social equal, and received the homage and honor due from magnanimity to her sex and her feebleness. And her enviable lot among us has resulted from two causes: the Christian religion and the legislation founded upon it by feudal chivalry.

How insane then is it for her to spurn these two bulwarks of defense, to defy and repudiate the divine authority of that Bible which has been her redemption, and to revolutionize the whole spirit of the English common law touching woman's sphere and rights? She is thus spurning the only protectors her sex has ever found, and provoking a contest in which she must inevitably be overwhelmed.

Casting away that dependence and femininity which are her true strength, the "strong-minded woman" persist in thrusting herself into competition with man as his equal. But for contest she is not his equal; the male is the stronger animal. As man's rival, she is pitiful inferior, a sorry she-mannikin. IT is when she brings her wealth of affection, her self-devotion, her sympathy, her tact, her grace, her subtle intuition, her attractions, her appealing weakness, and placed them in the scale with man's rugged strength and plodding endurance, with his steady logic, his hardihood and muscle, and his exemption from the disabling infirmities of her sex, that he delights to admit her full equality and to do glad homage to her as the crown of his kind. All this vantage-ground the "Women's Rights women" madly throw away, and provoke that collision for which nature itself has disqualified them, They insist upon taking precisely a man's chances; well, they will meet precisely the fate of a weak man among strong ones.

A recent incident on a railroad train justly illustrates the result. A solitary female entered a car where every seat was occupied, and the conductor closed the door upon her and departed. She looked in vain for a seat, and at last appealed to an elderly man near her to know if he would not "surrender his seat to a lady." He, it seems, was somewhat a humorists, and answered: I will surrender it cheerfully, Madam, as

I always do, but will beg leave first to ask a civil question. Are you an advocate of the modern theory of women's rights?" Bridling up with intense energy, she replied, "Yes, sir, emphatically; I let you know that it is my glory to be devoted to that noble cause." Very will, Madam," said he, "then the case is altered: You may stand up like the rest of us men, until you can get a seat for yourself."

This was exact poetic justice; and it foreshadows precisely the fate of their unnatural pretensions. Men will treat them as they treat each other; it will be "every man for himself; and the devil take the hindmost." There will be of course a Semiramis or a Queen Bess here and there who will hold her own; but the general rule will be that the "weaker vessels" will succumb; and the society which will emerge from this experiment will present woman in the position which she has always held among savages, that of domestic drudge to the stronger animal. Instead of being what the makes her, one with her husband, queen of his home, reigning with the gentle scepter of love over her modest, secluded domain, and in its pure and sacred retirement performing the noblest work done on this earth, that of molding infant minds to honor and piety, she will reappear from this ill-starred competition defeated and despised, tolerated only to satiate the passion, to amuse the idleness, to do the drudgery, and to receive the curses and blows of her barbarized masters.

The Consequences of Feminism on America as a Nation

Thus will be consummated that destiny to which so many gloomy prognostics point as the allotment of the North American continent: to be the accursed field for the final illustration of the harvest perdition, grown from the seedling of the dragon's teeth of infidel

Radicalism. God gave the people of this land great and magnificent blessing and opportunities and responsibilities. They might and should have made it the glory of all the lands. But they have betrayed their trust: they have abused every gift: above all have they insulted him by flaunting in his face an impudent, atheistic, God-defying theory of pretended human rights and human perfectibility which attempts to den man's subordination, his dependence, his fall and native depravity, his need of divine grace. It invites mankind to adopt material civilization and sensual advantage as their divinity. It assumes to be able to perfect man's condition by its political, literary, and mechanical skill, despising that Gospel of Christ which is man's only adequate remedy. It crowns its impiety by laying its defiling hands upon the very forms of that Christianity; while with the mock affection of a Judas it attempts to make it a captive to the sordid ends of Mammon and sense.

Must not God be avenged on such a nation as this? His vengeance will be to give them the fruit of their own hands, and let them be filled with their own devices. He will set apart this fait land by a sort of dread consecration to the purpose of giving a lesson concerning this godless philosophy, so impressive as to instruct and warn all future generations. As the dull and pestilential waves of the Dead Sea have been to every subsequent age the memento of the sin of Sodom, so the dreary tides of anarchy and barbarism which will overwhelm the boastful devices of infidel democracy will be the caution of all future legislators. And thus "women's rights" will assist America "to fulfill her great mission," that of being the "scarecrow" of the nations.

No-Fault Divorce Will Rise to Prominence Along with Feminism

A kindred cause, that of indiscriminate divorce, is making such progress in many States that it will soon be able to end a strong helping hand to its sister [the suffragette cause].

The Necessity that Men Embrace True Courage

Courage is the opposite of fear. But fear may be described either as a feeling and appreciation of existing danger, or an undue yielding to that feeling. It is in the latter sense, that it is unworthy. In the former, it is the necessary result of the natural desire for well-being, in a creature endued with reflection and forecast. Hence, a true courage implies the existence of fear, in the form of a sense, that is, of a feeling of danger. For courage is but the overcoming of that feeling by a worthier motive. A danger unfelt is as though it did not exist. No man could be called brace for advancing coolly upon a risk of which he was totally unconscious. It is only where there is an exertion of fortitude in bearing up against the consciousness of peril, that true courage has place. If there is any man who can literally say that "he knows no fear," then he deserves no credit for his composure. True, a generous fortitude, in resisting the consciousness of danger, will partly extinguish it; so that a sensibility to it, over-sensitive and prominent among emotions, is an indication of a mean self love.

The Battle Rages On

When the friends of the Bibles win a victory over one phase of infidelity, they naturally hope that there will be a truce in the warfare and they may enjoy peace. But the hope is ill-founded. We should have foreseen this, had we considered the real source of infidelity is always in the pride, self-will and ungodliness of man's nature. So that, when men are defeated on one line of attack, a part of them at least will be certainly prompted by their natural enmity to God's Word to hunt for some new weapon against it.

Responsibility and Justice

A man must be just before he is generous.

Appendix

Bibliography

The following works by Robert Lewis Dabney are published by Sprinkle Press and are recommended for further study on his life and letters:

A Defense of Virginia
Christ our Penal Substitute
Discussions, Volume I — Theological Evangelical
Discussions, Volume II — Evangelical
Discussions, Volume III — Philosophical
Discussions, Volume IV — Secular
The Life and Campaigns of Lieutenant General Thomas J. "Stonewall" Jackson
Practical Philosophy

About the Editor

Doug Phillips wears several hats. He is the president of The Vision Forum, Inc., a discipleship and training ministry that emphasizes Christian apologetics, worldview training, multi-generational faithfulness, and creative solutions whereby fathers can play a maximum role in family discipleship. The Vision Forum, Inc. is a San Antonio-based work dedicated to promoting the restoration of the Christian home through books and conferences. Each year they hold "Building a Family That Will Stand" conferences, apologetic boot camps, and father/son discipleship retreats in various locations throughout the United States. Doug also serves as adjunct professor of apologetics for the Institute for Creation Research, and as president of The Christian Boys' and Men's Titanic Society. He is a published author and a constitutional attorney who served for six years with the Home School Legal Defense Association. His most important "hat" is as husband to Beall, and father to seven children, Joshua, Justice, Liberty, Jubilee, Faith Evangeline, Howard Honor, and Providence.